OUR
WEDDING
ANNIVERSARY
JOURNAL

....
....
....
....

INTRODUCTION

Your wedding day is one of the most memorable days of your life, but what about the years that follow? Many of us have keepsakes from our special day, but the time you spend together as husband and wife is just as special and should be cherished. From family celebrations and amazing vacations to new homes and the birth of your first child, it's heart-warming to have a record of these occasions. Use the pages of this journal to create your very own wedding anniversary keepsake.

The first year of marriage is full of new possibilities, and as husband and wife you can treasure each of these moments in Our First Year Together, with room to write memories of your wedding, honeymoon, and first anniversary, as well as many other firsts. In years to come, you will fondly look back at these entries and see just how much you've grown together.

The Early Years and The Golden Years contain pages for you to write Significant Events and Hopes and Dreams for each anniversary. You may want to update each section as and when things happen or set aside a special time together around your anniversary to record all your news. As you enter your older years, your children and grandchildren will love flicking through the pages of this journal looking at old photographs and reading about your early life together—the perfect memento for future generations. It's also a wonderful keepsake for you both to look back on as you grow old together, giving you the chance to reminisce about times past and how your hopes and dreams have changed over the years.

Anniversaries

FIRST .... *paper*

SECOND .... *cotton*

THIRD .... *leather*

FOURTH .... *linen*

FIFTH .... *wood*

SIXTH .... *iron*

SEVENTH .... *wool*

EIGHTH .... *bronze*

NINTH .... *pottery*

TENTH .... *tin*

ELEVENTH .... *steel*

TWELFTH .... *silk*

THIRTEENTH .... *lace*

FOURTEENTH .... *ivory*

FIFTEENTH .... *crystal*

TWENTIETH .... *china*

TWENTY-FIFTH .... *silver*

THIRTIETH .... *pearl*

THIRTY-FIFTH .... *coral*

FORTIETH .... *ruby*

FORTY-FIFTH .... *sapphire*

FIFTIETH .... *gold*

FIFTY-FIFTH .... *emerald*

SIXTIETH .... *diamond*

What special memories do you have from your wedding day?

SHE

_____

_____

_____

_____

_____

_____

_____

_____

_____

_____

_____

HE

_____

_____

_____

_____

_____

_____

_____

_____

_____

_____

_____

Who gave the best speech? Was anything embarrassing said?

How many bridesmaids did you have? Were they all well behaved?

What was your best wedding gift?

SHE

_____
_____
_____
_____

_____
_____
_____
_____
_____
_____
_____
_____

HE

_____
_____
_____
_____
_____
_____
_____
_____
_____
_____
_____
_____

Where did you go on honeymoon? Did you stay in a special suite? What do you remember most? Did you buy anything interesting as a keepsake?

What's the first thing you did when you got back home from your honeymoon?

SHE

_____
_____
_____
_____
_____
_____
_____
_____
_____
_____
_____

HE

_____
_____
_____
_____
_____
_____
_____
_____
_____
_____
_____
_____

When did you host your first dinner party?
Who did you invite and what did you serve?

What's the first thing that really made you laugh as a married couple?

Did you spend your first Christmas at home, and if so, did you have family and friends over? How did you decorate your house?

What did you both do for your birthdays? Did you get any surprises?

SHE

HE

What's the first event you went to as a married couple this year?

Have you discussed having children, and if so, how many would you like and what would you name them?

SHE

_____
_____
_____
_____

_____
_____
_____
_____
_____
_____
_____

HE

_____
_____
_____
_____
_____
_____
_____
_____
_____
_____
_____

What was the last spontaneous thing your spouse did for you?

SHE

HE

What did you do for your first wedding anniversary?

Have you discovered anything new about each other in your first year of marriage?

SHE

HE

What's been your most memorable moment from this first year
of marriage?

SHE

_____

_____

_____

_____

_____

_____

_____

_____

_____

HE

_____

_____

_____

_____

_____

_____

_____

_____

_____

_____

SECOND

Significant events from the year gone by

_____

_____

_____

_____

_____

_____

_____

_____

_____

_____

_____

_____

_____

_____

_____

_____

_____

_____

_____

_____

_____

_____

_____

_____

_____

_____

_____

_____

_____

Significant events from the year gone by

Our hopes and dreams

Our hopes and dreams

THIRD

Significant events from the year gone by

_____

_____

_____

_____

_____

_____

_____

_____

_____

_____

_____

_____

_____

_____

_____

_____

_____

_____

_____

_____

_____

_____

_____

_____

_____

_____

_____

_____

Significant events from the year gone by

Our hopes and dreams

Our hopes and dreams

FOURTH

Significant events from the year gone by

_____

_____

_____

_____

_____

_____

_____

_____

_____

_____

_____

_____

_____

_____

_____

_____

_____

_____

_____

_____

_____

_____

_____

_____

_____

_____

Significant events from the year gone by

Our hopes and dreams

Our hopes and dreams

FIFTH

Significant events from the year gone by

_____

_____

_____

_____

_____

_____

_____

_____

_____

_____

_____

_____

_____

_____

_____

_____

_____

_____

_____

_____

_____

_____

_____

_____

_____

_____

_____

_____

Significant events from the year gone by

Our hopes and dreams

Our hopes and dreams

SIXTH

Significant events from the year gone by

_____

_____

_____

_____

_____

_____

_____

_____

_____

_____

_____

_____

_____

_____

_____

_____

_____

_____

_____

_____

_____

_____

_____

_____

_____

_____

_____

_____

_____

_____

Significant events from the year gone by

Our hopes and dreams

Our hopes and dreams

SEVENTH

Significant events from the year gone by

Significant events from the year gone by

Our hopes and dreams

Our hopes and dreams

EIGHTH

Significant events from the year gone by

_____

_____

_____

_____

_____

_____

_____

_____

_____

_____

_____

_____

_____

_____

_____

_____

_____

_____

_____

_____

_____

_____

_____

_____

_____

_____

Significant events from the year gone by

Our hopes and dreams

Our hopes and dreams

NINTH

Significant events from the year gone by

_____

_____

_____

_____

_____

_____

_____

_____

_____

_____

_____

_____

_____

_____

_____

_____

_____

_____

_____

_____

_____

_____

_____

_____

_____

_____

_____

_____

_____

_____

_____

_____

Significant events from the year gone by

Our hopes and dreams

Our hopes and dreams

TENTH

Significant events from the year gone by

Significant events from the year gone by

Our hopes and dreams

Our hopes and dreams

ELEVENTH

Significant events from the year gone by

_____

_____

_____

_____

_____

_____

_____

_____

_____

_____

_____

_____

_____

_____

_____

_____

_____

_____

_____

_____

_____

_____

_____

_____

_____

_____

_____

_____

Significant events from the year gone by

Our hopes and dreams

Our hopes and dreams

TWELFTH

Significant events from the year gone by

_____

_____

_____

_____

_____

_____

_____

_____

_____

_____

_____

_____

_____

_____

_____

_____

_____

_____

_____

_____

_____

_____

_____

_____

_____

_____

_____

_____

_____

Significant events from the year gone by

Our hopes and dreams

Our hopes and dreams

THIRTEENTH

Significant events from the year gone by

_____

_____

_____

_____

_____

_____

_____

_____

_____

_____

_____

_____

_____

_____

_____

_____

_____

_____

_____

_____

_____

_____

_____

_____

_____

_____

_____

_____

Significant events from the year gone by

Our hopes and dreams

Our hopes and dreams

FOURTEENTH

Significant events from the year gone by

_____

_____

_____

_____

_____

_____

_____

_____

_____

_____

_____

_____

_____

_____

_____

_____

_____

_____

_____

_____

_____

_____

_____

_____

_____

_____

_____

_____

_____

_____

_____

Significant events from the year gone by

Our hopes and dreams

Our hopes and dreams

FIFTEENTH

Significant events from the year gone by

Significant events from the year gone by

Our hopes and dreams

Our hopes and dreams

TWENTIETH

Significant events from the five years gone by

Significant events from the five years gone by

Our hopes and dreams

Our hopes and dreams

TWENTY-FIFTH

Significant events from the five years gone by

_____

_____

_____

_____

_____

_____

_____

_____

_____

_____

_____

_____

_____

_____

_____

_____

_____

_____

_____

_____

_____

_____

_____

_____

_____

_____

_____

_____

_____

Significant events from the five years gone by

Our hopes and dreams

Our hopes and dreams

THIRTIETH

Significant events from the five years gone by

_____

_____

_____

_____

_____

_____

_____

_____

_____

_____

_____

_____

_____

_____

_____

_____

_____

_____

_____

_____

_____

_____

_____

_____

_____

Significant events from the five years gone by

Our hopes and dreams

Our hopes and dreams

THIRTY-FIFTH

Significant events from the five years gone by

_____

_____

_____

_____

_____

_____

_____

_____

_____

_____

_____

_____

_____

_____

_____

_____

_____

_____

_____

_____

_____

_____

_____

_____

_____

_____

_____

_____

_____

_____

Significant events from the five years gone by

Our hopes and dreams

Our hopes and dreams

FORTIETH

Significant events from the five years gone by

Significant events from the five years gone by

Our hopes and dreams

Our hopes and dreams

FORTY-FIFTH

Significant events from the five years gone by

Significant events from the five years gone by

Our hopes and dreams

Our hopes and dreams

FIFTIETH

Significant events from the five years gone by

Significant events from the five years gone by

Our hopes and dreams

Our hopes and dreams

FIFTY-FIFTH

Significant events from the five years gone by

_____

_____

_____

_____

_____

_____

_____

_____

_____

_____

_____

_____

_____

_____

_____

_____

_____

_____

_____

_____

_____

_____

_____

_____

_____

_____

_____

Significant events from the five years gone by

Our hopes and dreams

Our hopes and dreams

SIXTIETH

Significant events from the five years gone by

Significant events from the five years gone by

Our hopes and dreams

Picture Credits

Polly Wreford
Front & back jacket, pgs 1, 5 below left, 6, 9, 11, 16, 20–21, 31, 39, 40, 43, 66, 69, 77, 81, 107, 123–4

Debi Treloar
Pgs 35, 47, 61, 65, 99, 112, 134

Caroline Arber
Pgs 3, 4–5 background styled by Jane Cassini and Ann Brownfield, 13, 48, 111/designed and made by Jane Cassini and Ann Brownfield

Carolyn Barber
Pgs 12, 18, 51, 95, 115

Claire Richardson
Pgs 23, 33, 74, 119, 120

David Brittain
Pgs 73, 85, 137, 144

Christopher Drake
Pg 52: owners of La Cour Beaudeval Antiquities, Mireille and Jean Claude Lothon's house in Faverolles; Pg 91: Maurizio Epifani owner of L'oro dei Farlocchi, pgs 109, 116

Michelle Garrett
Pgs 82, 92, 102, 143

Pia Tryde
Pgs 36, 70, 128, 133

Sandra Lane
Pgs 5 below right, 17, 44

Dan Duchars
Pg 5 above left, 5 above right

Peter Cassidy
Pgs 55, 62-Giorgio &

Ilaria Miani's Podere Casellaccia in Val d'Orcia

Craig Fordham
Pgs 2, 96

James Merrell
Pgs 7, 138

Chris Tubbs
Pgs 88–89: Toia Saibene & Giuliana Magnifico's home in Lucignano, Tuscany; Pg 100: a house in Maremma, Tuscany designed by Contemporanea

Ian Wallace
Pgs 58–59

Martin Brigdale
Pg 24

Melanie Eclare
Pgs 130–131: Judy

Kameon's garden in Los Angeles (designer & owner of Elysian Landscapes).

Catherine Gratwicke
Pg 86

Winfried Heinze
Pg 22

Caroline Hughes
Pg 78

Ray Main
Pg 56-Robert Callender & Elizabeth Ogilvie's studio in Fife designed by John C Hope Architects

Noel Murphy
Pg 127

Alan Williams
Pg 15

Designer Vicky Holmes
Senior Editor Catherine Osborne
Picture Research Emily Westlake
Production Gemma John
Art Director Leslie Harrington
Publishing Director Alison Starling

First published in the UK in 2009
by Ryland Peters & Small
20–21 Jockey's Fields
London WC1R 4BW

and in the USA
by Ryland Peters & Small, Inc.,
519 Broadway, 5th Floor
New York, NY 10012

www.rylandpeters.com

ISBN 978 1 84597 765 8

Printed and bound in China.